An Anthology of Poetry

By Mary Marriott

PublishAmerica
Baltimore

ISBN: 1-4241-3773-X
PUBLISHED BY PUBLISHAMERICA, LLLP
www.publishamerica.com
Baltimore

Printed in the United States of America

Introduction

My poetry is the result of a spontaneous spirit. No forethought, or hours of 'wonderings', just written as and when the subject or situation shows itself.

Acknowledgements

My warm thanks go to my sister, Lynne, for all her hard work in typing and searching for a publisher, to Louise, my daughter, for scanning the work, and to Gillian for her encouragement, as always. To Jacqueline for the invaluable use of her typewriter and Len, Julie, and Kim. And finally, PublishAmerica, thank you for taking me on.

London's Sloane Square

London's Sloane Square has an air about it, somehow different
from other Squares in London, perhaps familiarity on my part.
So busy with pedestrians, taxis, buses, private cars, though fewer
of the latter since they were forced to scatter as payment was
introduced by the London Mayor. London's Sloane Square doesn't
halt in its appeal to steal some hours to sit on a pavement chair
sipping wine not heeding time at all. Beeping taxis, slamming doors,
screeching brakes, aah! the risk one takes in trying to dodge these
moving vehicles to get to the other side. So cosmopolitan is
London's Sloane Square. A babble of talk wafts through the air
as characters walk passed, or ask. 'Excuse moi, eez zis taken, zis chair?'
or 'Puis je m'asseyer si vous plait?' The young are ordained in their youth,
not knowing in truth this time does not go on forever. It matters not,
as I too, give no thought amongst this lot of sparring humans to
the future. The wine is good, the buzz of life excites one to invite
others to enjoy time in London's Sloane Square, to sit and stare,
to drink in the atmosphere. A flower stall—a little pricey, but what of it,
don't think the flowers are dicey, after all, this is London's Sloane Square.
The occasional beggar passes by, having his eye on a bag or purse,
hoping, of course, he will not be ignored or cursed but handed a coin
or two. The Underground spews out people by the dozen, some alone, some
have company, and I imagine talking bubbles in the air and laugh at
unknown, unspoken thoughts and private conversations, some rude,
some silly, strange and funny. What a read, what fascination. And
coming from this basement some call hell, one used to hear the newsmen
yell, 'buy your paper here,' but now he simply stands and stares and waits
for them to go to him. Yes, some things die, tradition doesn't always
linger, no pointing finger, just a fact of life. Right next door, the theatre,
Royal Court in name, the one of fame, where actors old and new frequent
its stage, still the rage for theatre goers, adding to the atmosphere.
'Tis clear to see and feel the social intercourse charging through each one,
a force of intensity felt by theatre lovers. The hair salon, the wine bar near,

a bank, department store, though not rare, at least one doesn't have to travel
far, and just across the way, Kings Road, where young and old alike all delight
in shopping sprees. Cyclists as well, whose bells are as useless as a broken
light switch, darting in and out and round, and through, this fairground.
An air of confidence exudes in this place, quite extra-ordinaire,
the human race—in London's Sloane Square.

The London Chelsea Kitchen

Prices have remained more or less the same for years
in this in-expensive restaurant.
No elegance permeates the atmosphere, I fear 'tis not
a place for many of the human race, but I like it.
There's an ambience of laissez- faire and those that work
in service there, seem to care—all foreigners of course but this
is part of the ambience that invites one in to feast.
Well, not feast exactly but at least enjoy a simple meal,
perhaps with a glass of red or depending on how
one feels—white instead.
Its simplicity and lack of style causes me to smile.
I take a seat amongst the others, all chatting as they eat
spag-bol, lasagne, egg and chips, salad, baked spud
and beans that nip those hunger pangs.
Served hot (though this time cold) so being
bold informed the staff. Apologies expressed, food
heated up and the chips were free. You see, graciousness
abounds in a simple place like The London Chelsea Kitchen.

The Fly and the Spider

'Come into my web', said the spider to the fly,
'There's a human just behind you
And on you he has his eye.
A strange swatty gadget
He is holding in his hand,
I know it isn't me he wants,
So be careful where you stand.'

'O no thank you', the fly replied,
'I've heard of the likes of you,
Once you have me in your web,
I know what you will do.
You'll wrap your thread around me,
Then sting me so I'll die,
I know that I am food for you,
O spider, you are sly.

As he spoke, the gadget smacked him
Right across his head.
He hit the ground at such a rate,
There's no doubt that he was dead.
The spider shook, then lay quite still,
And looked upon the fly.
Should he go and pick him up?
It's a shame he had to die.

Slowly from the web he crawled,
And swung down to the ground,
The human that had killed the fly
Didn't seem to be around.
But as he went to have his meal,
Before he could escape,
a heavy boot did flatten him,
so the fly he never ate.

Oxford

The mere mention of Oxford conjures up imaginings
that stir excitement deep within. The whole idea
of viewing ancient buildings where academia is the
pinnacle of all that exudes from its walls is intoxicating
and worth pursuing. With so much to explore in this
ancient city, it would be a pity to miss out.
It lends an air of grandeur and of pride when walking
round its ancientness, pondering on the famous, the
infamous, the unknown, who studied and taught
between its walls. There is no doubt one easily falls in
love with Oxford city. It is also very pretty, with
Father Thames, (the Isis), flowing through its grassy banks
and trees which flank the water's edge. And in the spring,
fledglings sing their songs of freedom from their nests.
The bicycle takes precedence over other vehicles on the
road, for this is the students mode of transport and is not
at all absurd as some folk like to think. It's fun and fast,
and simply part of life in Oxford.
The Bodleian at best can only be entered on request.
Blackwells book store, no other in the land is quite
as good. Others need to take a leaf and put it in a book!
There is a modern part of Oxford city, 'tis not so pretty and
having dipped my toes in curiosity, I was not pleased
and felt impatient to escape this monstrosity of modern. My
spirit yearned immediately to leave as I observed this hell.
I hurried back to Oxford true and breathing deeply retraced
my steps and wandered through once more its ancient grounds,
and peace again descended.
The Inklings were a famous three who often met with friends
on Tuesdays in the Bird and Baby for a beer, or two maybe.
They also met on Thursdays in Magdalen for a cultured cup
of tea, when discussions thrived and feelings vented genius

into Narnia, Lord of the Rings, and essays by Charles Williams.
Lofty spires rising to the skies, tell of churches inspired and
built by men of old. The architecture leaves one breathless,
for in this day of lines and glass, modern buildings are so feckless.
Old has soul, holds it antiquity to its breast, how could
anyone detest such culture?
There are colleges to see within the boundaries of the university.
So much indeed to mention, but the intention is to say—go visit—
you will find this ancient place exquisite.

A London Station Café

A London station,
Main line to anywhere.
A café,
Coffee, please. Yes, white.
A table,
An ashtray with butts.
Given some satisfaction, I guess.
Dreary music,
Not in the background,
For the deaf.
Relieved to be seated,
I reach for my book,
Distraction at last.
But distraction of a different form takes hold,
The book lies unopened, limp, untold,
For next to me, two ladies gossip, loud,
And over by the door
Someone downs a pint,
Then walks across the floor,
Slaps down the glass, ne'er asks for more
But hurries out,
Content, for a mo. at least,
For pints of beer can be a merry feast.
A London station café,
A picture of a world within a world.
Outside, trains late,
Delayed, or simply stopped.
So the world within a world welcomes travellers,
Anxieties mopped—for a while..
The familiar refrain,
Coffee, please, No, black.
A hurried look around

And turning back
Pays his due and simply stands.
A comfort zone,
A place to sort out thoughts,
To write, to read,
Or just to sit, to stand,
Perhaps to plan.
Lovers in a corner kiss,
Not caring if their train they miss,
While others watching, listening.
Is their train next?
Some puzzling over crosswords,
some sending texts.
A buzz of conversation not audible to most.
Coffee, please, no, nothing else.
A dash, a wave, a fond caress,
Goodbyes, hellos,
Some pain, some stress,
All add to this world within a world,
Of a London station café.

Who'd Be a Bum by Choice

He sits on the pavement just near the hole in the wall. The majority pass
by laughing and talking, they don't seem him at all. Why should they?
They're having fun, not interested in a bum like him.
He stares at the pavement seemingly oblivious to everyone,
doesn't even try to make eye contact. A black shawl is around his shoulders,
his trousers are thin, his shoes the same—no designer name to gloat about.
How much will he 'earn' tonight, I wonder? Hopefully enough for a
drink and a bite to eat, and where will the guy sleep, not here, surely?
He'll catch his death, but most don't care, seems so unfair. There is money
sliding out of the hole, pocketed and pursed. Will he have cursed silently
either at them or his circumstances? What are his chances of housing, food,
clothing or even a job—pretty slim I expect as he is fobbed off too easily.
Perhaps he smells—his hair needs a wash and cut—who'd pay for that, or
even do it? Can't see him in some salon or barber shop, he'd be too embarrassed
to show his face to others of the human race. For someone on the street
it matters not to be clean and neat. It only matters to have food and drink
but would one think of buying him just that, instead of placing on his lap a
few coins that idled their time in a pocket or a purse, a curse to the rich who
just want to be rid of it. I know each coin adds up in order to buy that cup of
tea or bag of chips that nips the bud of hunger pain whilst sitting in the sun
or in the rain. What about a five pound note, what a surprise! Would he
believe his eyes and think it fake? Could he take a fiver to that hot-dog stall?
They may suspect he stole. So it's best to give him change, not re-arrange
his life causing added strife.
Is there a positive side to his life? How can there be in reality? Though no
mortgage, no bills to pay, no one to quarrel with over the ordinary things of
every day that make way for contempt and familiarity and so often closes
the eyes to sense and clarity.
I know I couldn't choose to be a bum, I would loathe the wet, the cold.
I'd miss my pillow and perhaps not be bold enough to sit and wait for the
odd coin from some passing folk Is this a joke? He has no choice, he has
no voice, he has no home to go to, like me, like you.
I'd miss being warm, would not want to face the storm of another day,
no certainty of what's to come.
Who'd be a bum by choice?

A Public Library

A public library was once a place of silence, whispers echoed
like secrets untold, and only walls could hold the private
conversations, and questions asked, put librarians to task to
search for books not found. The public was caressed by a quiet
that fed the inner being and at times, though not knowing, calmed
those who entered there. But now 'progress' has taken over and
computers line the tables which enables those computer literates
to tic, tac, tic upon the keyboards. Arousing my annoyance whilst
having a quiet read, I gave way to a vapour of intolerance for
the disturbance of my need to be quiet. I was informed—with
delight, I may add—that the silence requested was something of
the past and I had better now move fast else I would be left behind.
Libraries are no longer places of retreat where one once relaxed, by
putting up ones feet, metaphorically speaking, of course!
Sitting at a table, writing, no disturbance from a visitor or
'phone, alone in thought, no stress, besides it was a place of refuge,
away from the deluge of housework, shopping, children, husbands,
wives, a place to build on gaining strength, away from busy lives.
So now I take my refuge somewhere else, perhaps far better for this
stressful self. I walk along some country path and find I laugh when
thinking of my once reliance on a public library for quiet and peace,
but now I've found my niche in trees and fields and lying down with
book and pen, I lose myself in this quiet retreat from every public
gaze, from tic, tac, tics and eyes that raised objections to my
old-fashioned ways. The public library for me now, is to simply
take a look, grab a book, and run to find my fun, as I have said,
elsewhere, to be fed on sweet fresh air, far better for my health,
and I've increased in wisdom and in wealth.

Travel

To travel is to explore—it's either hated or adored.
'Tis an exciting way to get to grips with different cultures.
Understanding just unfolds with the thinking mind, for
travel broadens beliefs of a different kind to ones own,
unless one confesses to atheism, which, in a sense, is prison.
For not to believe in a Creator or Higher Being, is seeing
the world through dead eyes. You may not agree but you are
free, of course, to think what you will. I bear no ill
toward you!
Travel extends its riches in many spheres and so endears
me to its arms, its charms flirting with me all the way.
I have learnt to take its offerings in my stride, at times
like a roller-coaster ride.
I'll mention just a few, recommended to pursue, if life
presents an opportunity for you to travel.
Florence is an art, small, with magnificent appeal—it will
steal a little something from you.
Pompeii, crumbled to the ground, there is no sound, just
tourists drinking in the vastness of destruction.
Suave Paris with wide boulevards, cafes and the Seine.
Here one is caressed by all that's best and even streets a little
sleazy welcome you to take it easy.
The Himalayas boast the highest mountain in the world and
if you dare to travel there—beware! Its beauty is not spared.
Romantic Rome, a source of pride to all who live inside its walls.
Peter's Basilica, The Vatican, The Fountain of Trevi, where you can
throw those coins three, and eventually, all wishes will come true.
Monet's garden in Giverny, a splendid sight to see, with a
visit to his home where one may roam and feel the essence
of his presence in every nook and cranny.
Auschwitz is a must and though the dust it seems will never
settle down, for the world still wears a frown for what

happened there, when I walked its earth, God whispered,
"There is new birth—so go in peace and trouble not your
heart—for all is well."
When mine eyes fell upon the Valley of the Kings and Queens in Egypt,
an awesomeness, no less, caressed my all. This was a sight
beyond imagination, once a figmentation of the mind.

There's so much more. This is just a glimpse, a glimpse that
hardly satisfies, but nonetheless this tiny pinch should wake
you up from lethargy, and get you out to see the world through travel.

Don't Miss London

London is unique, it's ancient, quaint with narrow streets
and little pubs where people meet—like in all big cities.
The Underground, built before the First World War, so old,
parts updated but often fated with delays. Red buses are the norm,
some double up, some so long they take up half the road and
considered quite absurd. The taxicab is quite the fad, always
has been, this black machine. It's all part of London life.
'Incognito' is the name for those of us who have no fame to
shout about. There is no doubt this is the way to be, like ants
among their mud hills, scattering unobtrusively, each having a
part to play, not in disguise but unrecognised. Many people feel alone
and if they moan, best listen to the song—that if you roam
the streets of London, there will be something that will make you change
your mind. It's best to be kind to the beggars there who have no care for
anyone but themselves, for thirst and hunger wrack their bellies every day.
They have to sway your hearts to go into your pocket or your purse,
even if you have not known hunger or a thirst, you must give, not
count the cost. What will you have lost, I wonder?
The theatres call with flashing lights, telling all to take delight in these
atmospheric place. There are so many different faces, and cultures too,
who live and sleep in this old city, so inviting, daring, and
so pretty. Buildings old, tell a tale or two, dating back in history.
Ones built today hold a different sway lacking soul. Soul is the centre
of our being, so when seeing architecture
spread about in a way that is so cold, no hint of old,
London loses its appeal. But let us steal some time to look around and see
what can be found of interest. Near Old Father Thames, Big Ben, superb in
its display—a fine array of architecture. Then venture up Whitehall to
Number 10, now hemmed in by railings. Further on, we look upon Trafalgar
Square with old Nelson standing there. Then the Mall, which leads on to
Buck. Palace, where Chris. Robin went down with Alice.
Up The Strand past Charing Cross with the Obelisk. The Courts of Law
in Fleet Street grand, right into the City's land with St. Paul's offering its charms

with outstretched arms. We must not forget old Leicester Square where people stand and stare at those who shout the Christian message. Then down a narrow passage we find ourselves in China Town. Ne'er wear a frown, for it's fun to go there and join in the atmosphere of Chinese meals, and deals that aren't considered right, but freedom people choose their plight. Wander up Tottenham Court Road to Foyles, famous indeed for those who like to read. Next door, the West End, Oxford Street, far better travelled on your feet to take you down to Marble Arch and Hyde Park Corner, passing Bond Street on the left, which leaves the pouch bereft of every penny. So many places need a mention: Madame Tussaud's vies for attention, and Regent's Park, where with the squirrels one can lark. And don't forget the Zoo, will you. I think you'll get along just fine given time to see what London has to offer. Will take your breath away to feel and hear the atmosphere of this wondrous city. Many parts not cited, some perhaps a little blighted, but to be fair, these, too, add to London's air, its pulse athrobbing through each day and night. So take delight in your next visit, or if you haven't been before, then go along. I say don't miss it.

Traffic Wardens

Traffic wardens are a pain, so much so,
at times I wish for it to rain, not simply
rain drops sweet, but cats and dogs,
vicious ones at that, to nip the wardens
ankles or even feet, to tell them all to go
away and don't come back another day.
Law and order is a must, we all know that,
but surely flexibility is the crust we need
to feed upon—and trust.
There are the cranky motorists who do
not desist in parking on the doubles,
aware there will be trouble, but wanting
a fight, be it day, noon or night.
But for those of us who keep the rules,
at times we are the fools, for we take a risk
of a five minute dash to get some cash from
the hole, or drop in for a stamp, and coming
out find the car clamped. Not given a mo.
the wardens sure ain't slow.
I wonder if they have cars and find
themselves in similar plights, day,
noon and nights, needing to park on a
single or double or not having cash for the
parking machine and look around for someone
who can help out with change or exchange a
few coins for a fifty?
Got to be nifty to avoid these hawks who
continually stalk, come out of the drains
again and again, just there at the spot, not
caring a jot for you and yours, as long as they
write out a ticket—so wicked.
But we give them a job so I guess they'll
continue to log…

The M 25

The M 25, heavens alive, most travellers call it a hell, renowned
for its car parking facilities, in this it does pretty well. Housing
thousands of cars without a problem it seems, as people struggle
to work and rush to catch planes. Have to be at the airport three
hours before take-off, so that means an earlier start, whatever
the time. But there's always a need to watch the speed as
you drive, if you want to arrive in one piece, which, sadly,
so many don't do. At times there are break-downs which can't be
helped, it's the crashes that cause the car-park facility. So a lull in
the speed takes place to meet the need to slow down and stop.
Most times the traffic is halted for hours, which of course
causes rows. As they alight from their vehicles, strangers
greet one another, become like sister and brother, letting
off steam, furious that their dream holiday is now further away.
Perhaps they will stay overnight and wait for another flight
to Barbados. This sitting in jams is so common these days, that
it always pays to have taken a flask and a bite to eat, even a rug
to keep you snug when it's cold. Helicopters pass overhead and
land on the motorway, just behind or ahead, to pick up the injured,
sometimes the dead.
Those going to work—O, what a challenge EACH day many
would rather not have, takes so much to survive the M 25, but
there is no other way to get there. What stressful frustration we have
in this nation of too many people with too many cars, travelling near
and travelling far, causing so much pollution, but what's the solution?
For it's too late in the day to restrict immigration.
Yes, one has to be stoic, even heroic to stay alive on the M 25.

Ode to Timmy
(A Neighbour's Cat)

Timmy, you're gone,
It is hard to believe,
You've been around for so long,
Didn't think that you'd leave.

But you've left us with memories
That deserves you a mention,
For your pussycat ways
Always shouted attention.

You were bold, you were clever,
You were handsome and sly,
Thought you'd go on for ever,
Not choose to die.

We'll miss you, your antics,
Your neighbourly ways
Stalking and stealing,
A king in your day.

Farewell and thank-you,
For being half-friend,
Fearless and likeable,
Right to the end.

A Yob Society

'Tis such a shame that England courts a name and such a one of fame—
the yob society. A country once proud of gentlemen and ladies, now this
notoriety is fast fading. Youngsters of a different generation have grown
up with a freedom far too free, for one can see they are the walking dead,
fed on booze, contraception and each others bed. A freedom at its worst,
for though we boast democracy, its gone too far, and now the
youth are ill and lost in a titanic wave of self-gratification.
Yes, their agitation pointing to the centre of the 'I', a far cry from the youth of
yesteryear. Some say it is the generation gap, but I doubt that, for I believe
we have poisoned them with television, given in to the lack of discipline,
consequently they have no proper vision. An emptiness exudes from them
as they walk in the wrong direction. There's an infection that has carried
through, to children and to babies too.
I want to say, come on you yobs we love you really, for you are of the
human race, so why deface the world around you? Tin cans and
bottles have their place, most enjoy a drink of alcohol, but it doesn't have to
lead to hell. 'If', a tiny word as in Rudyard Kipling's poem—if this
were known—perhaps would bring back 'no', to discipline the young within
their souls. "You'd be a man, my son," the poet wrote, "If you can keep your
head when all about you are losing theirs and blaming it on you."
These words he felt in truth and ring forever true.

I Don't Believe in Magic Anymore

There was a time when I believed in magic,
I didn't seem to have a care at all.
I danced,
I sang.
I ran about so lightly.
Life was fun and full of laughter,
I never gave a thought to what might come after.
Today was just forever,
Enjoyed to its capacity,
Delighted just to see,
To hear,
To taste,
To touch,
To smell the roses,
All that life imposes on one,
If one believes in magic.
So why do I not believe in magic anymore?
Was I wrapped up in self deception,
An infection
Caught by those who welcome life with open arms,
Embraced by special charms?
Who knows!
This preciousness is gone,
And I live on with memories
That remind me how life was lived
When I believed in magic.

An English Country Tea Room

Trays of teas, large English scones,
pots of jam and cream, a stream of people
queuing, self service, choosing shortcake,
fruit cake, lemon drizzle, choc. gateau,
not sure what would be most pleasing.
Mouth watering, naughty but nice, perhaps
a slice of sponge. He who hesitates is lost
so take the plunge.
Seated with tea for two, we sit and watch and
wonder how on earth they got together.
Where did they meet? On the street? In a pub?
Perhaps a supermarket?
Between two others not one word is spoken,
no silence broken. Tea pot shared, a small
sip taken, digestive tract awakened.
A wry smile—not at anyone in particular.
What brought them here to this English
country tea room?
The buzz of conversation all around belies
the sounds within the confines of their minds.
This secret place where no-one else can show
a face.
There are those who chat aloud, no whispered
conversation, while others talk inaudibly,
just an observation, though some would comment
one was just being nosy, but no, humans are
so interesting, especially in this cosy
English country tea room.
Young couples with their children splendidly
behaved, no need for them to rave at all,
for special treats await their plates.
Bulging with strawberries and cream, they

only dreamed of an hour or so ago.
Sticky fingers gently wiped, in spite of protests,
'want to lick', 'not today, sweet one, now here's
a bun to finish off your tea with'.
Grandma's deaf, daughter raises her voice, so
we hear about the day they've had, the choice
of things to do and what and where and who. O dear,
one mustn't stare, t'is rude. It's hard to close
one's eyes and ears but, yes, it can be done, by
talking to each other in whispered tones.
Discrepancy at best—eyes down to rest the
senses which keenly take in all,
in an English country tea room.
The afternoon soon passes, trays collected with
empty plates and glasses. Jams and cream consumed
perhaps with dignity, but relish nonetheless.
One must confess to giving in to the delights of
goodies in an English country tea room.

There's plenty more, but enough is as good as a
feast, so I'll desist.

An Hour or So in a Local Café

A café in the High Street, not unique in any way, but pleasant in its
atmosphere where the chatter, so I've noticed, is constant every day.
Having spent time during the week, the odd Saturday, and
Sunday too, one would think the place be new, but it's years
since it opened up, and its good to pop in to have a cup—of whatever
the mind and body needs—don't have to feed. Customers
are greeted with a smile, payment and orders taken, and in a
while set down on the tables, where they are able to join the chatter,
or simply read the daily matter, a book or even write a poem, and if one
is known, pass greetings, a smile, a laugh. I wonder what sort of stories
all the chat would make if one could take them all together and write them
down?
Would they cause amusement, or a frown?
Four ladies in their dotage, gossip loud. Others seem
to talk of places been, some children actually scream,
and babies cry—I wonder why?
Some wear hats and keep on their overcoats which poses
awkwardness for holding knives and forks.
Others hang their coats on backs of chairs.
There are exceptions in this chatting game. One, no, two, today.
One alone, on the mobile phone.
The other far away in distant lands and cannot understand why people
laugh and smile, as all the while she is alone, alone with thoughts,
her grief and just below the surface a volcano rumbles. She knows
she mustn't stumble in this public place, so putting on a braver face says
hello to those sat near. A quiet rapport ensues, her spirit lifts, a smile then
gently sifts through this frozen face.
Perhaps she'll start again, and as the mist and rain lift up from her life,
the night will dissipate. This local café with its pleasant air, allows one time
to sit and stare.

A Candle for Kevin

Distant drums of the past echo in your mind,
Would death have been kinder?
Clutching at a straw, you clung to life.
It offered hope.
Dark days and nights ensued,
Anger, hurt, despair,
All part of the process of life
If you dare to hold on.
Hold on you did.
Perhaps inert in some respects.
Not ugly, scarred, yes,
Scars that remind you, and tell me,
Something happened that tried
To destroy you—but it didn't.
It is on the surface only,
The common gaze will fall.
Our lives are what goes on within.
Within the mind, the soul.
Your mind, it lives,
Your soul, it searches.
Dream, and you'll live another day.
For if you stop dreaming
You'll stop living.
But your candle is not extinguished,
It burns a light which says that you, too,
Are a light in this world,
An axiom of hope, indefatigable,
Not stagnating, but transcendent,
And giving to the world, your gifts.

Dedicated to Kevin, a friend and poet. Having been disabled in a car accident
he suffered severe depression and loneliness. He needed hope, and so I wrote
this for him.

Clear out Time

It's clear out time, though not yet spring
to herald in this annual thing
of disposing of and sorting out again.
Boxes crammed with precious items,
A 'holding on', too frightened to let go.
But the cliché says, 'move on'
and as I look upon my treasures of yesteryears
I remember.
It hurts too much to let that go
I remember how I loved him so.
Still do.
No, I'll keep that one for now.
Ha ha! and this?
What memories of bliss.
O my, is this really real.
Must they go?
I have to see it's best to hold them in my heart
where there's room for everything I wish to set apart.
O.K. this will go. But where ? let's see.
The dump or charity?
Perchance another soul could wear it.
O no, I really couldn't bear it.
So is it to the rubbish dump I'll call?
Bloody hell, I think perhaps I'll keep it after all.

British Rail

Slam, slam, slam. I hear echoes of slamming doors travelling
through my memory sphere, guardsmen shouting that all is clear,
passengers on board to journey home or perhaps to somewhere new.
Travellers were quiet and had respect for one another's space as they
sat on battered seats or stood on well worn stained floors dating
back to years before. Rattling wheels supporting rattling coaches,
squeaking brakes as the train approached each station. Sliding the
window down to reach outside for the handle and then a silent flurry
as people hurried to disembark, or come on board. Politeness reigned
as seats were offered to those who had the need to sit and bit by bit all
settled down to read or sleep. 'Tis quite a fascination to take a peep at
those who close their eyes, eager to find sleep to pass the time before
they reached their destination.
Alas, the world has moved on, 'progress' it is called, and the railway
sleep has been snatched away, for in this day of mobile 'phones and
lap-tops one is kept awake by listening against ones will, to
one-sided conversations, ringing tones that leave one bugged about
inventions, and the tic, tic, tic, as texts and emails are sent as quickly
and as frequently as a breath. The trains run smoothly now and have
sliding doors, no windows to reach for handles. Carpets plush and seats that
crush one up against the others. Yes, there is more space for bag and case but,
somehow, something's missing. I believe an atmosphere of yesteryear has
slipped out from our grasp as time moves on so fast, eluding us.
One cannot, must not, forget that British Rail too often failed in its
endeavour to get us there on time, particularly in bad weather. A leaf
upon the line caused grief untold and as for snow, this winter foe, it
brought delays, though inevitable, so unforgettable or perhaps I mean,
unforgivable!
One couldn't then phone home, so were alone in agony of being late for tea
and unable to inform those waiting—impatiently—at the other end.
British Rail was not our friend.
We hated you at the best of times, cursed you too and dreamt of travel new,

but now 'tis such a shame as we step on board the newer trains (all privatised)
with comfort, so called, at its best, the zest in me has waned as I look back with
nostalgia for those trains that caused us pain and even were quite vulgar.
Slam, slam, slam. That noise again. At least memories remain and, as long
as I am able to, British Rail, I will remember you.

O to Be a Child

Sweet child of mine,
A star sent down from heaven,
Perhaps divine, who knows?
Nine months to grow
Within a cave of darkness,
A cave of warmth and comfort,
A hiding place 'til birth takes place.
A scream, a shout
And out she floats
On board the boat of life
Where calm and strife
Will follow her along the way
And she will walk in peace,
At times to stray awhile
When no longer child.
But let us see
And know her innocence,
A gift bestowed
Upon the likes of this.
The gentleness of hands and feet,
A shriek of glee
When bounding on a knee
And in the bath,
We can only laugh
As water splashes in her face
And then the race to dry
Before the plughole swallows all.
Glug, glug, sigh.
The love, the trust,
A glowing from within,
She is bathed in innocence,
No sin.

Today is forever,
No yesterday and no tomorrow,
No thought of pain and sorrow.
Wrapped up in naivety
And tenderness,
She is caressed
By all who have the privilege of meeting her.
She stirs so many hearts,
Imparts the inner beauty of her soul.
O, to be as child.

A Roman Catholic Church

A Catholic education gave to me a fascination for Rome,
the home, we were told, for the pilgrims on Earth.
A home indeed, for the church met the need, the hunger,
the aloneness—all that is in the human soul.
On entering the sanctuary, this holy place of prayer,
one always bowed before the blessed sacrament, the silence
giving out a rare sense of awe.Kneeling before the Holy One
one hardly dare to show one's face, for this was the place of the
Holy Tabernacle and its awesomeness stirred the depths and
took away all anxiousness.
Silence filled the heart and mind, a kind of therapy took place.
Upon the heads of women, mantillas, black or white, crowning
them with stillness—an awesome sight. A Mass was said,
and rosary beads through fingers thread, tongues reciting quietly
prayers of faith. Confessions in the side chapels, lifted
souls from guilt and sin,so life could begin—again.
A blessing, then a penance, nothing desperately hard,
enough not to disregard ones' past. Then lighting candles would
take place to give thanks for new grace, or perhaps for prayers
for others in ones' care. Peace descended and
powerfulness all blended, within the confines
of a Roman Catholic Church.

An Hour or So in a Local Pub

A Guinness please, I'll have a wine. White, medium.
I think there's time before I have to leave. It will give
the courage that I think I need. The buzz of chat, an ambience
that one expects when ensconced within its eye, one cannot deny
expectation is fulfilled, sometimes without the realisation
of it all. Only when one gets up to go, having spent an hour or so
in this world of smoke and drink, a world that does not allow
one time to think about things that need to be thought about—
realisation kicks in. I believe it's called escape, but it's good to take
advantage of what's on offer, it's not as though one goes there
every night. No need to fight the conscience, just enjoy time out.
One-sided conversations on the mobiles often reach the ear and
as I listen, sometimes imagine the person on the other end,
family, or a friend, a lover wanting to discover what's going on.
Another pint, vodka or rum, come on, just one more glass. Please,
over there, just pass the ashtray this way—cheers.
Pretty girls and handsome guys all chatting, laughing, some in disguise.
A flattering look, a shy smile, 'May I have your number please,' is
often heard between the lines of conversation and at times a declaration
of that thing called love.
Sometimes a loner will walk in, perhaps with stubble chin. He stands
and waits his turn—a pint, a chaser follows on. What's wrong, I wonder,
in this life, so young, alone, has he a lady friend or wife? Has some
friendship come to a painful end? Who knows? I never will, for I'm a
stranger not a friend. Though if he wants to talk, stranger's ears are often
better than a friends but it depends on him. Perhaps he'd rather drown
his sorrows on his own and in doing so disown his pain until he wakes
tomorrow in his bed, to find another pain—this one in his head.
It's time to go. Goodbye. Hallo. I didn't see you there. Perhaps you'll come
again next week, if so, I'll buy you—what do you drink—a beer?

Road Works

Had to rush this morning, so much to be done, some of it fun,
some not so, but nevertheless I'll do my best to complete the
tasks by lunchtime. Turning the corner in the car, I could see
ahead, not too far, the traffic seemed to be at halt. O no!
A bolt shot through me as I knew, by experience of course,
and expectation, that this was just the beginning of trial, error,
patience, impatience, will power, calm tolerance, intolerance,
feeding myself on adjectives, positive and negative, but keeping
my objective in total vision. Having taken the decision to do all
that I planned, I mustn't allow them to be damned by road works.
Back into first gear and glancing in the mirror. I knew I was
not alone. Three vehicles make it on the green, two went on red,
and still looking ahead knew I would do the same. No-one to blame
but the absolute total inconvenience of road works. Pressing the
radio button, perhaps light entertainment would lighten the intensity
of irritability which seemed to cover me so suddenly. That in itself
is annoying, for I know calm acceptance, 'relaxez-vous' is best balm.
More minutes of my day have been eaten up, I guess I'll try the
short cut. No use, no space to turn, I felt my face burn. Someone isn't
on my side, in fact that someone seems bent on enjoyment at my expense!
Into second gear, mentally speaking that is, as I try to relieve the
tenseness that is relentless in its gathering within a short space of time.
More minutes gone, which way now? Keep going round the bend.
That's a laugh, I'm halfway there! Road works again and it starts to rain.
Blow! I've left my coat at home, just to help the mood along. Come on,
move on, please hurry, go through the red, they are only road work lights,
O dear, will I go home instead? Today is like my life, with mental strife,
that can only be dealt with calmly if one has a mind to.
A mile or so of peaceful driving, no anxiety or striving to be calm.
I should have guessed, another nest of cars, more road works.
Oh what a jerk I am, I said out loud, as another cloud descended on my
thinking.

Why bother to go out at all, this drives me mad. Have I become a sad
specimen of the human race? I need to pace myself
and not allow road works to get the better of me.
You see, no matter the necessity, they are a pain,
and I stupidly allow them to drain my equilibrium—how dumb!
Road works are dumb!

An English Country Pub

A fire blazing aside the hearth,
That chilly wind had set our path to find warmth
In an English country pub.
So welcoming this blaze,
To hark the chat and watch
As glasses raise to quench a thirst,
Or simply just to make a toast.
This ambience, this style,
Perhaps to know distress is worthwhile,
For so soon one is caressed
By all who fall into this country zest.
A glass of red,
A pint,
An orange juice with ice,
A gin with lemon slice.
The menu from the bar.
Spud au gratin,
Or salad at its best,
The rest is just as good.
Steak and chips,
Ne'er mind the diet today
Pub bad thoughts at bay.
A welcome chat from strangers,
Friends we had not met,
Laughter, smiles,
Perhaps to dim some pain,
Enough to gain new strength
To face what's cast aside.
Just an hour or so
With others of the human race,
Taking time and space,
To chill out,
In an English country pub.

A Short Break

He was leaning on the wall smoking a cigarette,
our eyes, they never met, for his gaze was fixed
across the street at the shop just opposite.
Attractive, in a cold sort of way but I guess
she made his day, for the look of him
uncovered his imaginings filing through his
thought zone.
Passing by nonchalantly, not casting an eye
until discretion allowed, I turned to spy openly.
One more puff, enough for a while,
and throwing the butt into the street, he took a
neat turn into his own shop until the next short break,
when, no doubt, he will fix his gaze in her direction,
no thought to a passer-by's detection.

An African Childhood

The vastness of the African plateaux
Was a scene of peace, stillness.
Thoughts of a childhood lived in freedom unsurpassed.
But unaware as children are,
Simply living, believing in the 'now'.
No questions asked,
Innocence protected.

Side by side, different colour, different culture,
Learning the lingo,
Tasting, drinking quietly, significant parts of each others lives.
Impostor? No thought of imposing.
No questions asked.
Innocence protected.

Cherished childhood days in a land of sunshine,
Bronzed bodies, bare feet, laissez-faire.
No questions asked.
Innocence protected.

Rhodesia—A Land That Was

There was a friendship between us,
We knew deep inside,
The white man and black man,
Had nothing to hide.

To their country we came,
To roam, to explore,
Our hearts were together
As they opened the door.

Through this door we could see,
A magnificent view,
A landscape of splendour,
A country so new.

The night sky was close,
And we reached for the stars,
One touched them, no doubt,
Saturn, Jupiter and Mars.

This land full of sunshine,
And yes there was rain,
So with nothing to lose,
There was so much to gain.

We worked side by side,
With our African friends,
Learning and teaching,
Together we'd blend.

Learning their language,
They learning ours,
We'd till, and we'd toil,
And then play for hours.

We taught them new skills,
From a different perspective,
And they taught us theirs,
Each became quite effective.

At times life was cruel,
Things seemed so unfair,
But we juggled and sorted,
For the main theme was care.

Respected and liked,
We grew close together,
Not always on a par,
But neither a debtor.

When push came to shove
We'd eye one another,
Perhaps disagree,
But shake hands like a brother.

Those days long ago
Were stolen away
By those that were greedy
And wanted their way.

Friendships were broken,
Mistrust crept within,
A land that was wholesome,
Now turned to sin.

The cry from their hearts,
Can be heard from the earth,
The white man and black man,
Their plea is new birth.

The greed it must end,
Else they all died in vain,
Can they be reconciled,
Live together again?

Mountain Pools and Waterfalls

(Growing up in Africa)

Sparkling water, like sparkling wine,
Finds the heart, the soul, the mind,
And cleansing fills the senses.
Freedom at its best
As the body plunges through the water,
Now caressed in and through,
Igniting all that one is.

Sensation tingling fresh anew,
Each plunge brings gasping breath,
Awakening the whole,
Renewing each sinew,
Muscle, aching limb,
Physical and mental,
Deep within.

These icy mountain pools that live
Their lives being filled
By cascading waterfalls
With penetrating,
Thunderous noise,
But bringing peace with such applause,
Appreciating its' own power.

Sunbeams burst through shading trees,
Allowing warmth and light, at times
A breeze to cool, while echoes of
Childrens' play ring throughout.
A scream, a shout.
Tides that cannot be stemmed,
This is freedom at its best.

Drat the Hat

(Growing up in Africa)

Bare feet was the norm,
Wearing a sunhat too,
But the latter irritated,
So I often went without,
Much to my own rue.
For sunstroke struck and laid me low,
That sunshine friend, and sunshine foe.
My father's shouts echo down through
Memory lane, so plain to hear,
"Mary, your hat."
"What's that?" I cried, pretending not to hear,
In fear I knew, to have to wear my hat.
O drat!

I knew I'd lie in bed for days
A sorry mite,
And angry at my stubborn ways, determined
To obey in days to come and not succumb
To sunny rays.
"Well again," I'd shout and out of bed
Once more to shaking fingers.
"Don't forget your hat,"
As I passed through the door of shame.
And so I'd wear my hat. O drat!
Until deliberately forgot once more,
And then, guess what?

Five more days in bed.
How careless of me not to dread this jail,
If only I could acquiesce
And humbly wear my hat. O drat!
I never did and suffered thus
For years.
Hats at school and hats at play
Were not my way.
But *they* knew best,
I must admit.
But as a child who wandered wild,
To wear a hat was simply not my style.
A hat? O drat!

Autumn

Lord, you took your paintbrush out
The other day, I know.
I see the colours in the trees,
There's a sparkle and a glow.
Your colours are so very rich,
So deep, so beautiful,
The very essence of Your love,
Is plain in such a skill.

The falling leaves, they wave goodbye,
Another season ended.
Your paintbrush moves across the sky,
Your graciousness all blended.
A flock of birds in silent form
You dab upon the blue,
A ray of light upon the green,
A wonderment of You.

No human artist can describe
In paint on canvas board,
The falling leaves, the gentle breeze,
Your creation, Lord.
With paint and skill and gifted mind,
He can create a picture,
But not like You, for Yours is real,
Countless times far richer.

Good Night

What is the point of staying in bed if you cannot sleep?
Seems quite ridiculous just lying there as the mind with all
its thinking keeps the self from sinking into abyss deep.
It's best to keep the light on or go down into the kitchen and
make a cup of tea, look outside and see if there is anything of
interest in the sky—it's far better than
to lie awake for hours. Even if there're showers, take a
walk around the block, have a bath, you'll laugh at your
antics in the night, but better this than putting up a fight
alone, struggling on for hours on end just lying there.
However, reading sometimes does the trick, helps to close
the eyes, or listen to the bedside clock's tick tick. The
radio has its charms, I've listened to a play and been
annoyed when awakened the next day to find I have
missed the plot and will never know what happened in the
end! It really sends one round the bend being able not to
sleep. A pill will only harm, so it's best you never take it
and really try to make on your own. A lonely time, but in
time you'll find yourself a cure, for sure. Why not try, not
to think about things any more, pretend life's just a blank,
nothing there to think about—and you'll have me to thank.
Good night.

Diana

From chrysalis to butterfly she opened up her wings and
spreading them, she flew, and angels heard her sing.
From little girl to womanhood she grew into a graceful
dove..A gentleness was hers and she caressed all peoples with
her love. Though 'tis said that beauty is skin-deep, with her this
beauty went within. How can anyone deny this beau ideal, our
Princess Di. She was chosen to be Queen, but her dignity, her loyalty,
her faithfulness all went unseen by some. Now truth in
death aspires and sets her free, and in this liberty her soul
lives on and leaves the races of the world much to ponder
on.
Diana, Queen of Hearts, you live within the hearts of all
who believed in you, and though we've said adieu, for sure
we'll meet again in your new world where judgement is but
God's, and God's alone.

Strolling Out

No matter what the weather be, to don one's coat and
walking shoes, to take a stroll, just has to be worthwhile.
One doesn't have to dress in style, just comfort.
A summer's day brings warmth upon the skin and hair and
fills the heart with not a care.
Spring is gentle, and one can spy new life peeping through
the earth as it gives birth.
Autumn brings a rush, a flurry, as if the trees are in a hurry
to wave their leaves good-bye.
It seems that nature wants to settle down a while as cold
take hold ushering in the winter bold.
To stroll down English country lanes, across the fields as
seasons yield their harvest, has to be the best of magic.
It takes away all insulation, stretches mind and body, no
limitation to the pleasures that it brings. One sings aloud
or softly hums and finds life easy to succumb to.
Strolling helps one be reflective, can bring one's life into
perspective, removes cobwebs of memories, refreshing
thinking like a breeze.
Once back home, one is not alone at all, as nature calls
persistently, for no other reason but for us to see the
glories of each season—when strolling out.

The Café Poet

She strolls down the High Street, thinking, deciding
which café will entice her into its warmth for a coffee
or maybe a light lunch, though she would have had
a hunch earlier, knowing within her mind, the place
she would want to write this day.
A bite to eat with glass of red which somehow fed
the appetite to put down on paper all that fills her senses.
Yes, the sights, the sounds, the smells, she can always tell
(or so she prides herself in) of what the people are about.
London is her favourite place to roam, through the city and
the nitty- gritty, down to the square called Sloane, to
Kings Road and Fulham Broadway she makes her way on
foot or bus, never in a rush, observing life as it passes round,
very little goes unfound. Summertime is fun, for with pad
and pen she sits outside Oriels in Sloane Square, and
always dares to buy that glass of wine, and sips for hours
at a time, drinking in the excitement of the Square, which
fills the air with something not quite tangible, though
something touches deep within her.
A bus ride from Sloane Street would take her up to
Kensington, where Harrods she'd explore. This store of fame
is somehow 'above the rest', but a coffee here is not the best.
The hair adornments are an exaggerated price, so do not entice
her to buy at all.
Another call to take near Brompton Oratory, a foreign café
here, where ordering scrambled eggs and bacon and a cup
of cappuccino, she settles down to read. Other customers
impose by talk and laughter, but of course this imposition
is a natural tradition, which creates the atmosphere in most
popular cafes. So senses full, the book she closes, herself
imposes by simply listening and observing. The foreign accents
lend ambience, so easy to embrace, so much so, she knows

she must come back in to this place near Brompton Oratory.
To the High Street once again to spend time amongst the locals,
and perhaps some tourists too, but now so few since nine/eleven.
Life somehow goes on, even when so many of the human
race are gone.
A café is her place of refuge, where she can show her face and
somehow feel at home, though at times alone in heart and soul,
on the whole she finds delight in this indulgence she
lends herself, this café poet.

The National Art Gallery

There is something magnificent about an art gallery. I recall the buzz
of excitement going on in my head as I made my way to the
steps leading up to the large doors which throw out a welcome,
and where I knew I'd be fed with genius. If I hadn't been for years,
I would wonder if Monet was still in the place where we met before,
to the right of the door, having passed through the shop selling their
lot of commercialism. I'd stare at the strokes on the canvas where
a genius who put them there comes back to life, exciting the senses,
feeling the love and strife that flowed through the brush or the knife,
from the heart, onto the canvas. I touch the passion of Van Gogh, his
sadness, which so many call his madness, bringing tears to my eyes
knowing that he went unrecognised in his time.
Constable in glorious England. The Renaissance, Impressionists all a wonder.
Rembrandt, Renoir, Degas, Sisley, Reubens, Turner and his Fighting
Temeraire, Cezanne, Seurat and not forgetting Toulouse Lautrec,
by heck, these masters cannot hide their brilliance. They bring a fresh
breeze into the modern stagnant mind that seems to have lost its soul.
Silence gathers momentum as the public file through room after room,
dispelling the gloom, casting eyes around, standing or sitting,
whichever feels fitting in the atmosphere of this gallery of art.
'Tis wonderful to be part of the scene, when once it was merely a dream.
I remember so well my first visit. I found it hard to believe that my eyes
received the original work of the great artists, not just an impression,
but the real amazing confessions of the souls of unique men and women
from so long ago. So, take it from me, don't be slow to get on your feet.
Infact run like a deer or fly like a bird, no I'm not being absurd—get up
to the gallery as fast as you can if you haven't before, something special
will knock at the door of your heart.

The N.H.S.

Three letters that once conjured up feelings of confidence,
relief, for having borne the grief of war, offered the comfort
of free hospital treatment for rich and poor alike.
There was no fight, no long queues and waiting lists and people
had titles—Mr. Mrs, and Miss. No familiarity, just respect.
Time was on everyone's side, with patient staff and personnel
conversation, eye contact, no tac, tic, tac on computer keys
that have removed all rapport and ease, that gave strength in times
of weakness, where distress was understood, and comfort given.
Now those not well are driven to distraction as waiting times are
longer, with no action taken for weeks or months on end. Seems
there is no friend amongst those working in the N.H.S.
So many have their senses closed, and others in authority impose
restrictions, withhold finance, and insist that cuts be made
in areas where it hurts the most.
Now our nation cannot boast of freedom to its own, for as
they bemoan the injustices put upon them, members of the
human race deface what was once held dear
and fear has crept in like a writhing snake,
and old values have disappeared without a trace.

Time

It's 4.45 am,
Time doesn't move on.
It's been a long 24 hours
But a week has gone.

Sleep evades, nothing unusual.
Thoughts travel far and wide,
Same, different, same,
Along paths—a crazy perusal.

Now wondering where, what, who and why,
Darting arrows through my mind,
The tiny clock ticks, ticks, no rhyme,
It holds our time.

The Job Centre and the Dole Office

I've been there—once—was shattered by
the attitude, so simply walked out. I've
ne'er returned, for memories of that short
time burn my mind. I've been told it ain't
improved a jot, so not to bother now to call
again, 'tis not worth the pain. Cards have
disappeared which used to sit upon the wall
advertising jobs—now there's nothing there.
You have to sit and stare at someone, ask
for what you want and the person scans the
tic tac tic—in front of you—no eye
contact or personable exchange. I can just
imagine it.
"No there's nothing here for you today,
perhaps you best come back another time
for me to re-arrange your life."
So, it's to the dole, what strife! There
I'll be forced to join the queue with others.
Am I a snob, for I fear I'll be robbed of dignity,
joining with the nitty- gritt?
Swear words, roughness, so many folk display
a kind of toughness that does not entice one
to be nice to them in any way. No
person is better than another, despite the
class we place upon ourselves. We are all of
the human race, so there is no need to
deface anyone with bad attitudes that cause
the feuds between each one. Perhaps life
would be simpler as a bum, to just compete
with others on the street by begging for that
thing I want to do. Maybe it's best to stay
at home, not roam the offices of the unemployed.
Yes, avoid the irritation, consider emigration.

London's Covent Garden

London's Covent Garden has air of surprise about it .Week-ends
of course, are the busiest, not necessarily the best, depends on
the mood at the time, but it's fine on a week day, quiet, with
stragglers, no hagglers to torment, apart from the odd 'big issue',
but they need a living, so it's good to be giving to the less well
off, after all, what's a quid or two—I know I wouldn't miss it
—would you?
There is the indoor market where the stall holders hope to sell
much of their wares, but at least they leave you alone to decide
for yourself, not like when travelling far from home, where
others of the human race are in your face, afraid you won't buy,
so they force themselves upon you.
There is fun to be had as silly people do silly things, pulling strings
to give a laugh and make you feel daft as some volunteer goes
forward for one act or another. The music players pluck their
strings and gently stroke their bows upon the violins. Masters
of voice bare their souls as they render love songs from
Bizet's Carmen, or, less passionate, a rendition of
The Flight of Little Men.
Pigeons strut from place to place as usual, but they are down in number
as the Mayor decided he didn't like them, so they had to find
other places for perusal.
Shops offer most things for the human race, of course depending
on your taste. There is a money making racket too, for those that act,
demand a price by sending round a hat. That's not so nice, for it's
greater to give when not asked to do so, but what the heck, here's a
pound for you sir!
There are jugglers in another square where crowds just stand and stare
and wonder at their dexterity, unique and O so neat!
One just laughs at all the fun and things daft in London's Covent Garden.
Scarves and jewellery galore, antiques, or, so they say, of 'yesterday'.
Different cultures performing acts of dance and magic, showing off an act

of humour or of tragic. Cafes dotted round on every corner, with menus on
the tables awaiting orders—of patisseries, wines, coffee, and of teas.
Cameras flash to hold memories to look back on in years to come.
Children clap their hands in time to the calypso and wide-eyed,
stare at scenes so rare.
Amazed it seems as if it were a dream all in disguise.
Applause and laughter fill the hall of entertainment, and echoes later on,
when all are gone, will be the only remnant of what was.
My feet, they tap to rhyme as I take time to sit and rest a while
and drink in the ambience of London's Covent Garden
Foreign accents reach the sense of hearing, some just grate,
while others so endearing, cause a smile and confirm in me
that a few hours spent in London's Covent Garden is so worthwhile.

The Café Rouge, just down the way, a favourite haunt of mine, is
where I spend time to partake of simple food, and, of course, a
Chardonay or Cabernet/Shiraz. One simply has an obligation to
oneself, a mild indulgence to quench the thirst of—well—self indulgence.

Separating Thoughts

It's good to filter through the tides of thought.
In fact one ought to do it regularly. For like
the sea, whose tides rush in and out, clearing,
sifting from what's underneath, discarding,
bringing in relief, a cleansing—so we too, should
sift our thoughts each day, throw those away
that steal our peace, find that niche on the gentle shores of life,
trusting energies that perhaps we fear. Tide and
time await no man, so as we sift through our
thought zone and learn to separate each thought
one from another, we will discover how to live
a fuller life, achieving, and in oneself believing.

Don't Throw Away Your Pearls

Pearls are such precious things and we know
that in growing them, the oysters suffer
painful stings—like giving birth. And so because
of this, 'they' say, don't throw your pearls away.
In other words, discretion speaks before one
leaks a magic tale to others. Always lend an
ear to test the tongue of sister, friend or brother.
It may take a while before one wants to share a
special smile or tear, but do not fear to hold it
in your heart alone, not impart a pearl at random.
If you do, the pearl may lose its specialness,
portray a sudden dullness which can never be
restored. Swine trample on and are unkind with
anything divine. So treat your pearls like secrets
(for that is what they are). Do not throw them out
with liberty, for you will see them crushed and you
will die within. Be strong, be bold and hold them
tight. They are yours by right, not mine, not theirs,
so keep them safe—like secret prayers.

Language

The Tower of Babel was the thing that sent mankind around the ring of mother earth. From birth (though Adam wasn't born, he was simply formed) man spoke one language and managed well. But because of vanity, God decided to confuse, perhaps also, to amuse Himself at mans stupidity, to see him loose his dignity, as he wondered round and round confounded by the sound of many tongues.

But now, languages are fine and useful things. It's great to have a fling at speaking different ones. Can be such fun. Can also cause distress and leave one in a dreadful mess if not conversant in any other except ones own, when far from home.

So many languages around the world all with different sounds, are a fascination. Is it my imagination that some are like Chinese or Greek or even double Dutch? There is such a clutch of puzzlements, one would think they had been invented! But of course, they originally intended to confuse!

Some are music to the ear, but some, I fear, are not at all endearing and can send the sense of hearing to despair.

It seems that mankind's history has nearly gone full swing, in that there is a language that is "number one". Right across the earth not some, but many kind of folk all speak their own and also 'number one'. One language is on the up again, it seems no confusion any more, perhaps God has forgiven, for, has man lost his vanity and is returning to how he used to be. I have a certain intuition (and without asking anyone's permission to say what I think!) man has become much worse, since the God who put the curse of different tongues upon him.

So what was the matter with God's plan to scatter man across the earth? I cannot see, for its all Chinese and Greek and double Dutch to me.

A Psychiatric Unit

I did a little nursing in my day, and on the way visited the Psychiatric Unit of a hospital. I was not at all enthralled with its appearance, its hospitality, and at best, supposed expertise at giving 'rest' to those who, either entered at their own request or were put between the walls at another one's behest. It was a hell, a quiet hell of sorts, where one could tell the sprits, hearts and souls of folk were not complete in anyway at all. Indeed, they just existed and I pitied them. Pity does not help, its pretty useless really, unless one puts it into action.

At times patients go out strolling, believing this will help to make them whole again, but when I discovered where they do this exercise, need I had been surprised?

There are car parks all around the grounds no prettiness is found, just grey cement, buses and cars exuding gasses, I lament. No ponds or lakes with ducks and birds, for goodness sake, what is this-some old fashioned institution? People rushing here and rushing there, no peace and quiet, the diet one needs for healing. This place is simply stealing from the inner being. No bird song, no butterflies to flutter by, no gentle breezes and no sky that gives one freedom. No open doors, no plants and flowers to look upon for hours to still the troubled mind. No waterfalls, no passive streams to give them dreams of peace and contentment, to know that soon the mess they're in will be dimmed and wholeness would have entered in.

Inside, locked up in units sickly green, with staff, faces stern, past caring. This is just a job, dealing out the pills and meals on wheels, making up the beds-these people too, need healing.

All souls need feeding with daily cups of sunshine, walks in a park or field, to yield to nature's course to make them well.

Recognition of the soul within each human being, is the magic that is healing.

The Mobile Phone

The mobile phone rings in the tone of modern living. It lends annoyance, amusement, indignance, an infringement on our privacy. It rings in church, when in the bath, one really has to laugh, especially when I heard it ringing in a desert, well, I thought, the world has gone to hell! I have one- old-and have been told that it should be discarded-put upon the shelf as one outdated, for as this goes to print, the phone is nine years of age-big and clumsy, some might say and, "Surely you can see its had it day, its time for you to catch up with the trend. Here, I'll lend you mine. Just try it out and see what fun's about!" Movies, photos, lots of tunes, and o so many ringing tones—some talk, some sing, one hardly hears the 'normal' ring—well, except on mine! And some are very rude! Recording too. I was caught out once just by chance, so must be aware of secrets shared.

Sending texts is the next best thing to talking. Abbreviations are the norm and have created quite a storm among the masters of the English tongue. But as long as youngsters know the spelling on their mobile phones are for them alone, no 'r's', no 'u's', no 'luv' and 'duc'. Remember English at its best, and never stoop too low to swap it for a 'mo' for 'texting language'.

I have often said "excuse me, pardon" to someone mouthing, walking toward me, only to discover he or she was conversing with another— on the mobile phone.

In bygone days, I declared that I would never have a mobile phone. I was staggered by its imposition and I stayed my course till my ear was bent and I was kindly given one—a useful present! I must admit, though it is a pain, intrusive is the name, it is a very useful gadget and I would find it hard to break the habit of it being in my life.

Just Incase

One person's rubbish can be another person's treasure, but not everything is made to last forever. Like tins of paint that have seen away the years and kept for—'just incase'—taking up the space that could be used for useful items. Rusty tools, not even fools could use. Their time has ended, cannot be mended. Pandora boxes holding things long past their date of usefulness and all leave such a mess of hopelessness. What's the point? Security is 'just incase', can't let go, need to know its in there, somewhere, doesn't matter where exactly, but, "I'll find it when I want it". Wellies as ancient as Wellington himself line the shelves—all different sizes, no surprises. Old fishing rods and spools lying with old garden tools, not seeing the earth since Elizabeth The First. Trainers too, 'just incase' someone needs a pair to wear when visiting. Who'd wear a pair of those old things for goodness sake, just throw them out and have no doubt you will not miss them. Bits of this and bits of that, all in the trap of 'just incase'. Feed them to the bins, there is no sin in throwing item that have had their day and now too old or broken up.

Just one more thing

Close your eyes and picture all empty spaces, now places new to store away, and a walk away through the garage or the shed to see ahead and not fear anything. A dream? It can be done, so have some fun in clearing out those 'just incases'.

The Rooster

She had grown tired of city life and wanted to move into the country where peace and quiet would be her longed for company. To leave behind the fumes, the noise, that destroy the health of body mind and soul was her ambition. There was a certain charm, she did admit, about living in the city. The park gave one a little quiet with seats that would invite her to sit a while and 'smell the roses'—that is—take time out from a busy life and simply 'be' that person one is supposed to be.
The garden of her home was really very pleasant and neighbours all around never made a sound that would annoy. Really, all was pretty fine but somehow there was no contentment in her soul and so she left behind the years of city toll.
The village that she moved to was so very quiet. She had her own drive which she never had before. Next door, a little church, was only open Sundays and the country lanes were only built for 'one way'.
The garden was so lovely and looked out on to the fields and each time she stood and stared a while she felt her sprit yield to say a thank you. Everything was magical, she didn't miss the noise or fumes at all. Parking for herself, no need to drive around the block to find a space—this used to drive her mad—but now life could never be so bad—
Until—her neighbours closely by decided soon to buy a ROOSTER. Enough said I believe, for a shock she did receive and her life is now in tatters and this noisy crow has shattered all her dreams.

Talk to the Hand, the Face Ain't Listening

Have you noticed in the last few years that a lot of people do not listen any more, it seems others are a bore? There is no interest in a two way conversation, they either blabber on incessantly about the 'I' or just stare on some pretext or another, or are they simply shy? If one dares to give some information of ones self, not indeed to hold complete attention, but to simply mention this or that, inducing friendly chat, their eyes glaze over, ears close up and before one knows it, they have shut one up.

I do not put all humans in this selfish category but must insist on this observation—that many folk now desist in making conversation. Talk to the hand, the face ain't listening, I was aghast but admit I laughed upon hearing this expression—but soon I heard an annotation of their views—we're not listening to you and don't want to.

What has happened to so many peoples of today—is this world wide this attitude that is so very rude and such a shame— I wonder who's to blame? In this particular society materialism has brought about the violation of the Laws that govern. Discipline has disappeared and children now are reared by parents doing as they're told. The plot's been lost and at such a cost, its quite incredible. The television leaves its mark, its mark indelible upon, not just the young, but older folk as well. It seems they're bound up in a hell, a whirlpool of deceit, worldly offer lifting them too high off their feet, so high they cannot see for looking at what cooking down below.

Holding doors allowing one to enter through is something of the past. No pleases, thankyous, yes or no, just grunts that leaves one feeling somewhat harsh towards those who have their hands before their faces. They embrace a different world, a world within this world with a gulf which now separates mankind from himself—not hearing, seeing, introspective, not reflective, can't be, for they cannot hear or see, just want to be without a face, leaving a trace of debris, as they journey on, lost it seems forever. Surely with endeavour they can be found again— if only they would lighten up, turn off the noise, unplug the ears and listen to the silence in their souls. There is time for them to be made whole.

Man's Inhumanity to Man

Can one ever understand the full extent of mans inhumanity to man—gutless men and women inflicting sever pain as punishment on other natives of the human race? More than simply, a disgrace, 'tis a mockery of man, born above all other creatures, even higher than the angels.

Since time began, it seems that man has been at war against himself. Power is their need and this extends to greed and wanting to be better than all others, so they smother, extinguish those who propose to live in peace.

Auschwitz and Birkenau are constant reminders of mans inhumanity to man, lost its face, as millions proclaimed, "My God, why have you forsaken us?" For, forsaken they were in their hour of need. No one to plead for them at all. Cold blooded monsters, not only took the lives of helpless human beings but tortured them for being who they were.

And so man continues to wend his way today, and if spared, tomorrow he will persist in the abomination of slaughter in every nation of the universe. It is a curse, must be, put upon the man who wants to rule. His heart does not beat with love but with cruel intention to dominate, exterminate and to own, then sit upon his throne.

Rather than feel undermined, men do not submit but with determined grit, retaliate to over come the enemy. They do not see it's all the same—man's inhumanity to man.

Words

'Sticks and stone may break my bones but words will never hurt me', a cliché that resounded through the playground of my youth, at times vibrating an uncouthness in the voice.

But words can say and mean so much, can be a gentle touch or create a storm that says too much.

Sticks and stones could never really break the bones as was implied, but words can break the heart, the soul, and words can help to make one whole again.

Silence too, can talk, and feel we ought to use this way of telling others that we're listening, more often. Silence frees and sends a breeze of understanding. Words can over-spill and not until it's far too late, if something wrong's been said, that one may realise that there are times one must be quiet instead.

The tongue is just the instrument, for words come from within, where silent battles rage and gentle thoughts, and then flow forth upon the stage of life.

Words build up or destroy, depending how they're used, so we mustn't toy and be blazé, for once spoken, words can never be retracted, in fact once we've given them away, we may not say they're ours—they've gone and to other do belong.

So it's wise to keep our counsel when using words.

Printed in the United States
57241LVS00005B/490-492

9 781424 137732